That's What
Love
Is For

Stormie
Omartian

HARVEST HOUSE
PUBLISHERS
EUGENE, OREGON 97402

That's What Love Is For

Copyright © 1998 by Stormie Omartian
Published by Harvest House Publishers
Eugene, Oregon 97402

Library of Congress Cataloging-in-Publication Data
Omartian, Stormie.
    That's what love is for / Stormie Omartian.
        p.   cm.
    ISBN   1–56507–914–0
    2.   Love—Religious aspects—Christianity.   I.   Title.
BV4639.057   1998
241'.4–dc21
                                                98–4071
                                                    CIP

Design and production by
Koechel Peterson and Associates, Minneapolis, MN

This book contains true stories, but in some instances the names have been
changed to protect the privacy of the people involved.

98 99 00 01 02 03 04 05 06 07 / DR / 10 9 8 7 6 5 4 3 2 1

This book is dedicated to

Michael, Christopher, Mandy & John

who have taught me
to experience love
in greater depths than I
ever thought possible.

Contents

There are three things that remain— faith, hope, and love—

and the greatest of these is love.

—1 CORINTHIANS 13:13

That's What *Love* Is For

A few years ago my husband, Michael, and his friend, Mark Mueller, wrote a song with the title I have chosen for this book. Amy Grant also contributed to writing some of the lyrics and recorded the song on one of her albums. "That's What Love Is For" was an enormous success because hearts resonated to its message.

The lyrics speak of the way love smoothes the rough edges of our lives and gives us strength to keep going forward. It reminds us that when all seems lost, love can change everything for the best. And isn't that what we all want? Love that is strong, selfless, unwavering, and unconditional. Love that fills us with joy, grows us up, carries us through, strengthens our hearts, and gives us hope. Love that is life changing. Surely that is what we desire. And why not? After all, that's what love is for.

$\mathcal{L}$ove
Responds with Patience and Kindness

$\mathcal{T}$hose of us who have experienced love in great abundance see acts of love everywhere, and we expect love to be given and received in equal manner. We can easily *give* love because we've *been* loved. And we find it easy to respond to others patiently and kindly with love. Those of us who have felt deprived of love often find ourselves searching for it in every face that passes. Our fragile hope is mixed with the fear that love won't be there now because it wasn't there in our past. Most of us probably travel somewhere inbetween these two worlds, having known enough love to believe it's there to be found, yet needing assurance that we won't grow old without it.

I often observe the elderly because I seek to pattern my coming years after those I most admire, the men and women who always have a ready smile, kind words, and a genuine interest in those around them. In short, these people have love to give and are willing to give it without a thought of it being returned. One elderly lady, forever imprinted upon

Wherever there is a human being there is an opportunity for kindness.

–Seneca

my memory, showed me how even the smallest act of kind and patient love can make a world of difference.

"LOVE IS VERY PATIENT AND KIND..."

As a public speaker, I am often invited to speak to groups of women at conferences and retreats. On one weekend in May I had just finished speaking to a large audience and was talking with a sizable group of women who had formed a loose line in front of me. A small, elderly lady with a kind face had been waiting patiently in the line, but her advanced age prevented her from standing on her feet any longer. She walked up past everyone else and gently but firmly placed her hands on my arm. Then she closed her eyes and smiled a big, tender smile.

The young woman who was talking to me at that moment was holding both of my hands, so I couldn't touch the elderly lady in return. I simply looked over at her and gave her a smile, assuming she had come to say something to me and was waiting until the young women had finished talking to me. But the elderly lady didn't say a word.

After several seconds, she opened her eyes, squeezed my arm, continued to smile, and  walked away. As I watched her go, I felt an unmistakable sense of love penetrate my entire being.

I never saw her again, nor did I find out who she was. But I won't ever forget her or what she did for me. I believe in my heart that this woman was praying for me, and in that brief moment I had sensed a reassuring combination of her love for me and the overwhelming love of God. This small, elderly lady required nothing in return—not even my acknowledgment of her presence. I had never before seen an act of love so simple and yet so powerful.

I learned from her that each of us always has *something* to give. And the most important part of that giving is that it's not necessarily *what* we do; it's what's in our hearts when we do it. The simplest act of love, done with a kind and patient heart, can profoundly bless and bring wonderful things to another.

Small things done in great love bring joy.

—Mother Teresa of Calcutta

Love is

a sacrifice

a loyal heart

a warm smile

a generous spirit

a choice we make

an encouraging word

an expression of kindness

After my mother died, I frequently called to check on my elderly father. But one morning he didn't sound very well.

"Dad, you sound terrible," I said.

"Oh, it's nothing. I'll be fine," he responded feebly.

"We're coming up to see you," I insisted. "Just rest until we get there."

After I got off the phone, my husband and I and our two children packed up the car and made the four-hour drive to Grandpa's. Upon arrival, we bounded in the door with bags of groceries, goodies, and medical supplies, but Grandpa couldn't even get up to greet us. He had a bad chest cold and a severely sprained foot.

"Dad, I'm going to make you a big pot of chicken soup, and we're all going to take care of you," I said.

All through the weekend, I and my family fed Grandpa, cleaned his house, administered vitamins and medicine, doctored his foot, and—best of all—talked and laughed with him. By Monday, he was a new man. None of us ever recalled seeing anyone get well so fast. And that gave us an idea.

"Dad, we want you to come live with us," I said. "We want to be able to see you every day."

Grandpa moved in. He just celebrated his ninetieth birthday in good health. Love is truly the best medicine.

That best portion

of a man's life,

his nameless,

unremembered acts

of kindness and love.

—WILLIAM WORDSWORTH

Love has an
amazing law of return.
If we give love,
it will come back to us
by some means or path.
We don't get to choose
how it will come back,
but there will always
be a compensation
far greater than
what we've given.
And it may
only be in eternity
that we will reap
its full consequences.

Love
Accepts Others

*L*ove blossoms when we reach out in acceptance of others, thinking the best of them, believing in them, and putting their needs before our own. But when the weeds of negative thoughts begin to crowd out love's fragrant blossoms, we risk losing carefully cultivated love.

Jealousy is one such weed that squeezes out love. It grows wherever seeds of resentment are planted. The psalmist asks, "Who can stand against it?" The answer is no one, for jealousy can bring down anyone standing in its path. We should be thankful when we are forewarned of its coming, for we are then blessed with the opportunity to eliminate its presence from the garden of our heart.

If we choose to embrace love and faithfully care for it, weeding out any jealousy that might overtake it, we will experience the rewards. If we don't, love has lost a home.

"LOVE IS...NEVER JEALOUS OR ENVIOUS."

When I was in college, I roomed with a girl who was beautiful, talented, intelligent, popular, and wealthy. I looked at her, then looked in the mirror of my mind and believed that I was none of these things. By focusing on myself and making a daily comparison with her, I let a seed of jealousy take root in my heart.

Even though I liked and admired this girl very much and valued her friendship, the initial seed of resentment that I  allowed to sprout eventually created a permanent barrier between us. And although I was careful never to do or say anything that showed my envy, I know she must have felt it, perhaps without even realizing exactly what it was. It kept us from being the close friends we could have been, and after we left college we never saw or spoke to one another again.

When I was married I found myself immersed in my successful record-producer husband's lifestyle. In this life I found myself surrounded by beautiful, talented, intelligent, popular, wealthy, and *famous* women. By this time, however, I had a personal relationship with God and had grown in receiving His love for and acceptance of me. I was also now able to recognize a jealous spirit for the harmful thing that it was.

One afternoon I was forced to make a decision that would forever change my life. At a gathering in my home, I suddenly realized that every woman present had all of the attributes I admired and desired. As I began to compare myself to each one of them, I became smaller and smaller in my own eyes until I was nearly invisible with intimidation. I knew that if I didn't do something to stop it right then, envy would eliminate all chances I had of developing meaningful relationships with these women in the future. I recalled what had happened between my roommate and me, and I wanted a different ending this time.

I had a choice to make. I could let my insecurities determine the outcome, or I could stop focusing on myself and the exterior qualities of these women and instead choose to view them through the eyes of the God of love who had created them in His image. I decided to choose God's eyes.

"Lord, I know that comparing myself to others is pride," I prayed silently. "I don't want that or the envy that comes with it. Change me and help me to love others the way You love them."

Something did change in me at that moment. I became free. Free to appreciate others for who God made them to be. Free to be thankful for *their* blessings without weighing them on the scales of my heart to see whether theirs were balanced with mine. It was a turning point from which I determined never to stray.

I know that this kind of experience is not exclusive to me, for who isn't tempted from time to time to harbor a jealous spirit? The cause of it doesn't even have to be based in reality. But when we invite the love of God to fill our hearts, it crowds out jealousy so effectively that the unwanted emotion finds no place to rest. The love of God enables us to love others at a depth we otherwise could never know.

This story, like all stories of true love, has a happy ending. Each one of those women became a close friend of mine and remains so to this day. No walls. No barriers. And I've learned what love and envy have in common. Both require effort, and both can turn into something big. We always have the freedom to choose one over the other. Sometimes the greatest act of love is simply to resist that which would destroy it.

Love
brings us joy
clears our minds
gives us courage
fills us with hope
lights up our darkness
strengthens our hearts
lifts us to heights we've never
imagined

Tom and Patti had been married for several years before they finally saved enough money to buy their first house. Along with the down payment, they had placed enough in their savings account to be approved for their loan. Every penny was tight.

One morning Patti's estranged stepmother, Janis, called them and asked to borrow five thousand dollars.

"I don't know if we can lend money to you at this time," Patti said. "You see, we're trying to buy a house, and we need every dollar in the bank to make sure our loan is approved. But I'll talk to Tom about it."

Patti immediately called her husband and told him the situation. "What will happen if we lend her the money?" she asked.

"We might not qualify for the loan and lose the house," Tom replied. "On the other hand, we might lose any hope for a reconciled relationship with Janis."

After more discussion and prayer, they decided that showing love to Janis and restoring the relationship was far more important than the house.

Patti called Janis, told her of their decision, and sent her the money. They knew with all certainty that they had made the right choice.

The very next day they received a check for five thousand dollars from an entirely unexpected source.

"Can you believe this?" Patti exclaimed.

Within a week they purchased their first home.

In the years that followed, Janis was generous to Tom and Patti in ways that far exceeded the amount she had borrowed. She bought them things for their new home and later helped pay for their daughter to attend private school. Most of all, their relationship was restored to a new wholeness that might never have happened without an act of selfless love.

Love is the doorway through which the human soul passes from selfishness to service and from solitude to kinship with all mankind.

—Anonymous

Love Humbly Cares for Others

Unselfish and noble acts are the most radiant epochs in the biography of souls. When wrought in earliest youth, they lie in the memory of age like the coral islands, green and sunny....

—Rev. Dr. Thomas

$\mathcal{A}$ common trait among us is that we often believe our opinion is right while another's is not. This belief can make our relationships difficult to maintain, because often we are faced with situations where our beliefs don't harmonize with someone else's. And we can become boastful and proud in these instances, proclaiming our correct position while giving no listening ear to the other side. This makes it difficult for us to live peacefully with others, much less love them.

Yet when we love, we no longer need to prove that we are right simply because we think we are. And even if we are right, sometimes the more loving thing to do is to humble ourselves and let the other person win. More often than not, our selfless actions will light a similar candle in their heart, and we will arrive at a place of understanding. Even if nobody is declared the "winner," love will make everyone feel like one.

"LOVE IS...NEVER BOASTFUL OR PROUD..."

My son Christopher was four when my daughter Amanda was born. From the time she could crawl, she adoringly followed her big brother everywhere and worshipped the ground he walked on. And he, in turn, was crazy about his baby sister.

As they grew older, Christopher became more and more involved with school and friends and consequently had less and less time for Amanda. Deeply hurt, she frequently became upset with him. And he would react with less-than-pleasant results.

I found myself constantly pouring the water of reason on their heated squabbles. One day I decided that I'd had enough of their bickering. I jumped into the middle of an argument between the two and demanded that  they immediately stop fighting. I then informed them that I needed to speak with each one of them alone. First Christopher and I went into another room to talk.

"Chris," I said. "Why are you fighting with Mandy?"

"Because she gets mad at me when I don't play with her," he replied. "She doesn't understand that I have other things to do."

"You're right," I told him. "You do have other things to do. But I think if you were to look at things from your sister's side, you'd understand. It's not always easy, but sometimes you need to let Mandy have her way because you love her. Just be willing to say, 'You're right, Mandy. I do need to play with you. Let's figure out a time when we can.' I think that would help her to know that you still care about her."

He agreed to do that and then went out to send Amanda into the room to talk with me.

"Chris won't play with me anymore," Amanda succinctly explained her side of the story as tears streamed down her cheeks. Her heart was broken over this issue, and she wasn't reluctant to let anyone within earshot know all about it.

"You're right," I told her. "Chris does need to play with you. But take a look at things from his side. Because you love him you need to be willing to say, 'You're right, Chris. You do need to spend time with your friends. But can we just set a time when we could play?' I think that would make everything work out."

She nodded her agreement and we went in to talk with Christopher.

"How do you want to settle this?" I asked them.

"I do want to play with you, Mandy," Christopher said. "Let's set a time to play together."

"I know you have other friends, Chris. So let's set a time," Amanda replied.

They agreed on a good time, and I was grateful not to hear any arguing for at least a week. Then both of them had an apparent lapse of memory, and we had to have the conversation all over again. But the seed of understanding had been planted, and they were willing to work at their relationship.

To me as a parent, it was obvious what happened when my children humbly responded to each other's needs. Humility made the other person feel loved, and because of it they were able to work through their difficulties together.

Love is

not giving up

simply listening

being transparent

bearing another's burden

reaching out and touching

giving with no thought of a return

showing compassion for the

suffering of others

And now this word to all of you: You should be like one big happy family, full of sympathy toward each other, loving one another with tender hearts and humble minds.

—1 Peter 3:8

The only things
we do on this earth
that will bring
life and last
for eternity

are the
things we
do out of love.

$\mathcal{S}$imple Acts of Love

When our children were small, my husband and I worked at home. We had a treasured saying we found necessary to keep repeating to each other: *Remember, love is letting someone help you even when you can do it better by yourself.*

Countless times one of us would call across the house to the other, "Please remind me what love is again!"

This was a signal that one of us was trying to get some work done, but it was taking far longer than expected because one of the children was "helping." The person responding would either come to the rescue and divert the "helper" into performing another important task, or simply quote the treasured saying with an understanding smile.

We learned that acts of humble and sacrificial love happen when we include someone else in our lives, even when it would be far more convenient not to do so.

Love
Notes

Love kindled

by virtue

always kindles another,

provided its flame

appears outwardly.

—Dante Alighieri

Love produces love.
The more we love,
the more we are
capable of loving,
and the more we will
feel the love of
others toward us.
An act of love
is like a stone
falling into a lake.
The ripple effect
goes on and on...

Love
Gives with Compassion

I remember times when I was new in a neighborhood, a town, a school, a job. During these moments of uncertain beginnings, I often felt invisible, not known or understood, maybe not even liked. And these were the moments when I searched most for understanding eyes and words of kindness. I looked for a friendly smile or even simply a glance of recognition. And when nothing came, emptiness and loneliness did, along with a lump in my throat that held back a river of tears. All it would take was one gentle touch of a hand on my arm, a moment of friendly eye contact, any semblance of love, and the river would begin flowing and my suffering would be appeased. I could finally smile at life again.

Reaching out to touch a stranger is an act of love we can't afford not to offer. All it requires is a small gesture of compassion, a tender word that shows we are willing to give of ourselves to bring happiness to another person. Sometimes it takes so little to change our world.

"LOVE IS...NEVER HAUGHTY OR SELFISH OR RUDE."

Slumped in an aisle seat at the back of a crowded airplane, I waited for takeoff. As I glanced toward the front of the plane to try and determine the reason for the delay, I saw an elderly African-American lady painstakingly making her way down the aisle with only the aid of an old walker. She trudged and clattered one step at a time through first class, but when she reached the coach section she realized that her walker was too wide to fit in the narrow aisle. She folded up the metal contraption and held it with her left hand while she used her right arm to brace herself heavily on the back of each seat she passed. Slowly placing one feeble foot in front of the other, she struggled for balance as the line of travelers behind her bobbed with impatience.

"Why doesn't someone help her?" I sighed with exasperation.

I was certain that someone close to her would lend her a hand, but no one did. The passengers in seats near her continued to read their newspapers or silently witness her struggle.

My heart ached for this woman as I remembered the many times I, too, had been a lone traveler, handi- capped by the weight and volume of burdens  too great for me to carry alone. How I longed for someone to reach out to me. How it hurt when no one did.

"What gives you the right to criticize others for not helping when you're doing the same thing?" I rebuked myself. "What makes you any different or less rude than they are?" The reality of having no ready answer to my questions propelled me out of my seat and down the aisle. In an instant I was by the woman's side.

I took her walker in one hand and her arm in the other, and together we walked to row 17. She struggled with all her might to hold onto my hand as I lowered her into her seat, and her face showed great concern when I gave the walker to a crimson-clad flight attendant.

"That lady in the red sweater will get the walker for you whenever you need it," I reassured her.

She had not spoken a single word during our brief encounter, but she now looked at me without any change of expression and smiled with only her eyes. In that instant, without any doubt, I knew I had seen the face of God.

Don't think only of yourself. Try to think of the other...too, and what is best for him.

—1 Corinthians 10:24

*Love
makes us whole
gives us purpose
inspires hope to try again
heals our body, soul, and spirit
meets our ultimate human need
cares about the welfare of others
gives us strength to get up when we fall*

My young daughter once informed me that she didn't ever want to have children.

"Why not?" I asked incredulously.

"Because I would have to change their dirty diapers. That would be disgusting," Amanda replied with great certainty. "How do parents do it? How did *you* do it, Mom?"

"Well, I didn't think about *what* I was doing. I thought about *why* I was doing it."

"What do you mean?" she asked.

"I mean, I thought about how much I loved you and how I wanted to do whatever was best for you. When you love someone, you're aware of their discomfort and you do what's necessary to make them feel more comfortable. Love enables us to do things we never thought we could."

She pondered my answer for some time until it seemed to find a resting place in her heart. Soon after that I observed her openly admiring every baby she saw. I felt a great relief. Maybe someday I *will* be a grand-mother, after all.

Love
Seeks the Best for Others

When I think of the things in my life I deeply regret having done, or the things I have left undone, one common thread links them all together—a distinct lack of love on my part.

In making peace with my past, I have examined the times when I was not mature enough to make good choices or not wise enough to know the best way to live in order to make life really work. I have apologized to those whom my inconsiderate or unloving words, attitudes, or actions may have hurt. But when I think of people to whom I cannot apologize or make amends, I long to go back in time and change my actions.

That not being possible, I have done what I can do. I have prayed that the love of God will bless these people in ways I never could. And I also pray that when I have opportunities to show love I will respond rightly, seeking the other person's best.

"LOVE DOES NOT DEMAND ITS OWN WAY."

I was in my mid-twenties and living in Los Angeles when I landed my first commercial. Because it was for a flower care product, we filmed it on location at some of the gorgeous fields of flowers outside the city. I drove my own car to the shoot so I could keep the many different outfits I would need for the day's work hung neatly in the backseat. On the floor, in carefully arranged cases and bags, were all the accessories that went with the clothing. The director rode with me as I drove the short distance between each location, and we talked about the setup of each upcoming scene.

The cameraman brought his seven-year-old son along with him that day. While the director and I drove, the two of them walked from location to location carrying the father's equipment. We had been filming since dawn, and sometime in the afternoon  the cameraman asked me if his son could ride in my car for the rest of the day. Blinded by my own needs, I did not see a tired and hungry little boy who needed my attention and love. I saw a wiggly kid with muddy shoes and dirty hands who had the potential to ruin my entire wardrobe and possibly, along with it, my career. I saw someone who could break my concentration and keep me from focusing on my lines for the next scene. Instead of words like "kindness" and "caring" being my motivators, my mind resonated more to words like "interruption" and "inconvenience."

"There's not enough room," I responded to the cameraman's question. "I'm sorry."

"You heard what she said. There's not enough room," he repeated my words to his son. "You stay with me." He turned and walked off, and I could see the disappointment on both of their faces. It bothered me a little at the time, but I had convinced myself that I must be careful not to do anything that would jeopardize my future.

We finished filming and I never saw the cameraman or his son again.

A few years later, I met someone else's son. God's. And I read His love stories in the Bible. As I did, I came face to face with a love so powerful it transforms lives, tears down barriers, helps us rise above our frailties, and makes us better than we could ever hope to be on our own. I came to know the real thing and, as a result, grew very aware of what was counterfeit in my life. When I asked God to cleanse me of all that was not of Him, I was given a clear picture of the loveless things I had done and was shown how they significantly contrasted to His ways. I saw that every time I had demanded my own way, or sacrificed another's needs for my own, I had lost something valuable. I saw that whenever I didn't show love, I was the loser. I saw the cameraman's little boy, and I wept.

I still regret my lack of love for him on that day. He is a grown man now and most likely has a family of his own. I pray that God will pour His love on him in all the ways I never did. I hope that he has long forgotten the incident. I know that I never will.

Love is

keeping a promise

knowing when to let go

rejoicing with those who rejoice

believing for the best in someone

accepting others for who they are

taking time to really know a person

making a sacrifice only you can possibly make

The supreme
happiness of life
is the conviction that
we are loved.

—VICTOR HUGO

Simple Acts of Love

Lou took his prized bow collection down from the wall, leaving just his three favorites. He had spent nearly twenty years collecting, polishing, and painstakingly caring for the bows. Aside from his family, of course, they were his most valuable possessions.

His daughter, Stephanie, would celebrate her sixteenth birthday on Saturday, and Lou wanted to do something special for her. Stephanie had sacrificed so many of her summers babysitting for her younger brothers while Lou and his wife worked hard to support the family. He wanted to repay his daughter in some way. She needed a car to get to work and to school, but the family could not afford to buy another vehicle.

Lou picked up the phone and dialed Jim, his old archery buddy. "Everything's ready," he said.

"Are you sure you want to get rid of those bows?" Jim asked. "It's a beautiful collection, and I know how much they mean to you."

"I'm sure," Lou replied. "Just keep *your* part of the deal." He hung up with a grin.

When Stephanie woke up on Saturday morning, her dad said, "Happy birthday. I'm sorry we don't have your present yet." Seeing her disappointment, he added, "But we'll have it very soon, and I promise it will be worth the wait."

Later Stephanie saw Jim's shiny red car in the driveway.

"Dad, isn't that Jim's car?" she asked.

"Not anymore," he replied. "It belongs to someone celebrating a sixteenth birthday."

"Are you serious?" she squealed in disbelief. "It's mine? But how did you buy it? Where did the money come from?"

"Don't worry about that," Lou hugged his daughter. "You deserve a car."

Later Stephanie realized that her dad's prized bow collection was gone, and she was deeply touched by the sacrifice he had made. She could never doubt that her father loved her very much.

Love Notes

Never miss a chance

to love when

it is offered.

What you get back

will sustain you

forever.

—C<small>HRISTOPHER</small> R<small>EEVES</small>

Something done
for another
out of love
is not easily forgotten.
It stays in the heart
and only eternity
will know its
consequences.

Love
Is Easy to Get Along With

Love can change a life, a nation, or the world. But sometimes we hesitate to show love because we don't realize how important our love could be to others. Or we don't want our love to be interpreted as anything other than what it is. Our intentions to love might be good, but as our actions play out in reality the results often fall far short of what we had envisioned ourselves accomplishing.

Many of us yearn to be like Mother Teresa and go to the soup kitchen every day to feed the poor. In reality, however, few of us are able to make the same type of commitment she did. But why not try to be a Mother Teresa in our own environments? In our own homes? In our own neighborhoods? Why not give all the love and compassion we can right where we are? What better place to start changing the world?

"LOVE...IS NOT IRRITABLE OR TOUCHY."

The day my family and I moved into our new house, the seller warned us about the woman who lived next door. "She has been in and out of mental hospitals," he said, "and is, shall we say, *different*."

This was immediately confirmed by one of the workmen who was painting the kitchen. Using this unique neighbor's name in an unfortunate alliteration, he said, "Psycho Sally is angry at everybody—especially anyone who lives or works in this house."

I thanked them both for the information and vowed to do my best not to offend her.

As it turned out, however, I didn't have much opportunity to follow through on my promise. Early the next morning, Sally was in our front yard yelling so furiously that it was difficult to make out what she was saying. I gathered she was angry because our workmen had rinsed their tools with a hose in front of our house, and the water had run down the street in  front of her house. Without stopping to allow me to apologize, she went on to describe in full detail the many offenses people who had previously lived in our home had done to her. She concluded this one-sided conversation by saying emphatically, "I didn't take it at the institution and I'm not going to take it now," and stormed off.

I knew we were in trouble.

I went to the neighbor across the street to tell her what had happened, hoping that she could give me some suggestions about how to handle future encounters with Sally. She told me that many people in the neighborhood had had similar experiences with her. And she offered some insight into this troubled woman's background.

"Sally was badly abused as a child," the neighbor explained, "and ended up in a mental institution. Her parents owned that property, and when they died she inherited it. She moved in after she was released from the hospital but was angry that someone had built a house next to hers."

I immediately realized that my unhappy next-door neighbor was suffering from deep feelings of being unloved. Having learned that the best way to combat animosity is through a peace offering, I returned home and put together a big basket of fruit, cookies, cheese, crackers, and candy. I wrapped the basket up in pretty pink cellophane and tied it up with ribbon, then placed it on her front doorstep with some flowers and a note that read:

DEAR SALLY,

WE ARE YOUR NEW NEIGHBORS NEXT DOOR AND WE WANT TO APOLOGIZE FOR WHAT THE WORKMEN DID. WE ARE SO SORRY THAT YOU HAVE HAD SUCH BAD EXPERIENCES WITH PEOPLE WHO HAVE LIVED OR WORKED IN THIS HOUSE. WE DON'T WANT TO BE THAT KIND OF NEIGHBOR TO YOU, SO WE PROMISE TO DO EVERYTHING WE CAN TO SEE THAT THOSE THINGS DON'T HAPPEN AGAIN. PLEASE ACCEPT THIS BASKET ALONG WITH OUR REGRETS. LET US KNOW OF ANYTHING YOU SEE WRONG AND WE WILL CORRECT IT. WE WANT TO BE DIFFERENT FROM WHAT YOU'VE EXPERIENCED IN THE PAST.

Much to my surprise, the very next day we received a note from her. It simply said:

THANK YOU FOR THE BASKET.
NO ONE HAS EVER DONE
ANYTHING LIKE THAT FOR ME.
—SALLY

Sally only complained a few times after that, and on each occasion we acted in love to try and right the situation. Our other neighbors later observed that when Sally walked her dogs, ours was the only property where she didn't allow them to leave their "calling cards." I smiled to myself, amused, yet amazed at the far-reaching effects of a single act of love.

Love is

not keeping score

not passing judgment

forgiving over and over

not taking things personally

giving the benefit of the doubt

not doing it again after you apologize

taking someone's past into consideration

You must love the Lord your God with all your heart, and with all your soul, and with all your strength, and with all your mind. And you must love your neighbor just as much as you love yourself.
—Luke 10:27

43

Love doesn't always

have to be

a great commitment

of undying devotion.

It can be a simple

moment of compassion

for another human being.

*Kindness
is the insignia
of a loving heart*

—E.C. MᴄKᴇɴᴢɪᴇ

Love
Forgives
One Another

Kind words of forgiveness are like beautiful flowers. They bring happiness when they are given and their effects can last a lifetime. They brighten our minds, bring a renewed fragrance to our souls, and forever change the course of our lives with their essence.

Kind words should also be chosen carefully for the right occasion. But they must always be given with love, lest they become nothing more than a sound that accomplishes little which is good or lasting. If words are laced with forgiveness, kindness, mercy, and love, they can make the difference between faith and doubt, peace and strife, or joy and sorrow. Long after loving words cease to be heard by the ear, their message resonates loudly in the heart.

"LOVE…DOES NOT HOLD GRUDGES AND WILL HARDLY NOTICE WHEN OTHERS DO WRONG."

"Have you seen my gold bracelet with the three little diamonds on the front?" I asked my husband one morning. "The one you gave me for our anniversary? It's not in my jewelry box, and I've looked everywhere for it."

"No, I haven't seen it," he replied with concern.

Our home wasn't so big that something as valuable as a diamond bracelet could easily be misplaced. I knew it had to be somewhere in the house because I had worn it the weekend before and distinctly remembered taking  it off and putting it back in the jewelry box on my dresser. I hadn't seen it since then, but I had been busy with our six-month-old baby and had plenty of other things to think about.

When I didn't find the bracelet over the next few days, I grew more and more concerned.

One afternoon someone knocked on our door. It was Sara, the thirteen-year-old girl who lived two blocks down the street. She seemed very nervous and asked if she could come inside and talk to me. I had not spoken to her very much before and could not imagine what this was all about.

"Are you missing a bracelet?" Sara asked.

I was completely shocked to hear the question come out of her mouth. She had never been to our house before, and I had told only my husband about the missing bracelet. How could this girl possibly know about it?

"Yes, I am missing a bracelet," I said. "Why do you ask?"

"Because Sandy next door has it," she replied. "I've known about it since she took it and have felt so bad that I couldn't sleep. It's on her dresser in a little glass dish. If you go ask her mom to look in her room, you'll find it. But please don't tell Sandy I told you."

I couldn't believe pretty little fourteen-year-old Sandy, our sweet babysitter who lived next door, would do such a thing. I had always been so kind to her. My shock turned to hurt, and then to anger. *How dare she do that to me?* I thought as I walked next door to talk to Sandy's mother. *She's going to have to learn a difficult lesson.*

Without mentioning Sara's name, I asked Sandy's mother to please look in the glass dish on her daughter's dresser to see if my bracelet was there. She asked me to go with her, and I was happy to oblige. When Sandy's mother lifted the little glass lid, there was my bracelet. It looked odd to see something so familiar to me in such an unfamiliar place.

Sandy's mom immediately broke into tears, then proceeded to tell me how her daughter had been caught shoplifting in department stores a number of times. This, however, was the first incident where she had stolen from someone they knew. I was stunned to hear this about Sandy because she didn't seem the type to do such things. She came from a nice two-parent family with plenty of money. Why would she steal? And why would she steal from someone who cared about her and trusted her?

"When Sandy gets home from school, I want you to have a serious talk with her. She must be punished for this and she doesn't listen to me," said her mother.

I assured her I would have plenty to say, then went back home.

In the few hours that passed, my heart changed. I knew that if something lasting were to come from this discussion, whatever I said would have to be out of love.

At four that afternoon my doorbell rang and there stood Sandy and her mother, both looking very sad.

"Sandy has something to say to you," her mother said.

"I took your bracelet the night I babysat for you," Sandy said without looking at me and with no emotion whatsoever. "I'm sorry." She steeled her face for the harsh words she expected me to say.

"Sandy," I said, "I want you to know that I forgive you. I care about my bracelet, but I care more about you." Sandy looked at me for the first time and tears came to her eyes. "It hurts me that you don't know how valuable you are and how much you are loved—by me, by your parents, by your friends. It grieves me that you don't see your own beauty and gifts and abilities, that you don't know you have a bright future ahead."

As I continued on, she put her face in her hands and began to sob. I talked to her for close to an hour about how God had created her for great things and how, as much as we all loved her, God loved her even more. When I ended the conversation by praying for her, I saw a ray of sunshine emanating from her face. She smiled broadly and promised she would never steal from anyone again.

My family moved from that neighborhood not long after that, and I didn't see Sandy for a number of years. One Sunday afternoon I was at a large church picnic when a young woman holding a beautiful baby boy came up to me. I didn't recognize her at first until she told me that she was Sandy, my former babysitter.

"I turned my life around after we talked," she said. "Your words made such a difference to me that day. I couldn't believe that you could still love me after what I did. It made me never want to do wrong again. Now I have a wonderful husband and a new son, and we go to this great little church. I just wanted to say thank you."

I gave Sandy a big hug and told her she had made my day. The truth was, she made more than that. Twenty years later, I am still reaping the rewards of choosing words of love and forgiveness instead of words of judgment. Every time I think of Sandy, I will always feel joy.

Love

comforts

is more than a feeling

means being responsible

gives us a vision for the future

shows mercy instead of judgment

is the foundation for all lasting change

helps even when it's unpleasant to do so

Jenny and David had been married for five years and Jenny was deeply concerned about their relationship. They had been arguing quite a bit lately over issues that were not as serious as the arguments made them out to be. Jenny remembered how David used to frequently send her flowers and little notes. Now it seemed like he only thought of his business, his friends, and his activities.

That night Jenny slept fitfully. She woke early in the morning with feelings of sadness and dread. She slipped out of bed and knelt down on the floor, crying. "O God, please make things right between David and me," she sobbed. "I really want our marriage to be happy. Show me how to be a better wife to him. If I'm the one who is at fault, change me. If he is, convict his heart. Please open the communication lines between us and help us to understand one another. Fill our hearts with *Your* love and change us."

She got back into bed, fell asleep, and didn't wake up until she heard David's voice. She opened her eyes and there stood her husband with a breakfast tray in his hands. "I brought you something to eat. All your favorites—strawberries, fresh-squeezed orange juice, scrambled eggs, toast with honey, and tea," he said proudly, placing the tray on her lap and fluffing up the pillows behind her.

Breakfast in bed was Jenny's favorite thing. She looked at the food so carefully prepared and served on the good crystal and china. A rose from the garden sat in a little glass vase, and beside it was a note that said simply:

I'm sorry. Please forgive me.
I love you,
David

"How could I *not* forgive you after seeing this tray?" Jenny said as she touched his hand. "I do forgive you. Will you forgive me, too?"

"It's done," he said. And truly it was.

"Thank You, God," Jenny whispered. "This is better than I even had hoped!"

Love Champions the Truth

Nothing but love will heal the wounds of our world. Every day, people fight for the causes of truth and justice but always seem to come up short of having enough love to make the kind of changes that are lasting.

You and I *can* change the world, though. We can *give* love. And the love we give in a day will multiply far beyond what we could ever imagine. It will flow through the lives we touch into the lives *they* touch, and on and on love will go—serving, healing, saving, forgiving, sustaining, and transforming.

And truly, that's what love is for.

"LOVE...IS NEVER GLAD ABOUT INJUSTICE, BUT REJOICES WHENEVER TRUTH WINS OUT."

Tears poured down Roz's cheeks as she shared her heart.

"I don't belong in this group," she sobbed. Her face was beautiful even when she cried.

Roz had been a part of our Tuesday morning women's group for more than a year. All six of us were close friends who got together weekly to discuss the important issues of our lives and pray for one another. I could see by the looks on everyone's faces that they were as stunned by Roz's comments as I was.

How could Roz feel this way? I thought. *We all love her like a sister. She is a kind, godly, talented woman who has a successful husband and a wonderful son. They live in a great house in the same neighborhood as the rest of us, and we all go to the same church. What possible reason can she have for saying this? How can she believe such a lie?*

"Roz, you belong here as much as any of us do," I said. The others spoke in profuse agreement.

Only Susan sat silent for a moment and then said, "I think I know where this is coming from. And I know what we need to do. This may sound odd, but I believe we need to apologize to Roz on behalf of our ancestors' racial prejudice. I feel there is a deep hurt in Roz because of the cruelty and indignity she has suffered in her past as a member of the African-American community. These feelings need to be healed. Let's prove to her how we really feel."

All of our hearts resonated to Susan's suggestion, and we unanimously decided what we were going to do.

We took Roz into our master bathroom, which had a huge square-tiled tub built down into the floor. Each of us took off our shoes and sat on the wide flat-tile rim around the edge of the tub. One by one we stood in front of Roz, filling our hands with the water that trickled out slowly from the brass faucet, and washed her bare feet. As we did, we apologized to her for any hurtful things the people of *our* race had done to her, her family, or the people of *her* race. We spoke the truth to her—which was we loved her and she belonged in our group as much as anyone.

First went Debra, who was Jewish. Then Priscilla, from Hispanic heritage. Next came Susan and Lisa, who were from the South. And I, who had come from a part of Los Angeles that was a hotbed of racial strife, went last. All of us had seen or experienced the devastation of racial hatred. We knew well the wall that needed to come down. And we were convinced that love was the tool by which to do it.

And come down it did. Roz broke down and sobbed from the depth of her being. Each one of us had our own tears mingled with the cleansing water. They seemed to wash away a lifetime of pain and suffering.

After that day, Roz was different. Great healing manifested openly for all that she had long suffered in silence. She became more outgoing and confident in herself and her abilities. She had always been a great singer but did not often sing in public. Even though she had accomplished many significant things, there had always been an insecurity in her that kept her from fully enjoying her triumphs. Now she began to sing openly, growing bolder and more secure each time.

Just recently I heard Roz sing again. In her voice I heard no fear. Only freedom. Life flowed out from her to the hundreds of people who listened, and her success was unmistakable. As I watched her, I recalled the foundation that had been laid years before in one heartfelt show of love. It was a day none of us will ever forget. The day when love reached out to bring the truth that transformed a life. The telling of it can't begin to do justice to the powerful dynamic that transpired. It forever changed us all.

Love
opens doors
builds bridges
tears down walls
fills in the empty places
smoothens the rough edges
opens a window to the soul
lays a solid foundation for trust

All love is sweet,
given or returned.
They who inspire it most
are fortunate...
but those who feel it most
are happiest still.

—PERCY BYSSHE SHELLEY

There is no
greater feeling
than that of knowing
we are loved.
It enables us
to fly, to soar
on top of the world,
to endure anything.
It is the source
of all joy.

Love Always Encourages

We have it in our power to change lives every day, especially the lives of those who are closest to us. We can strengthen or weaken their self-worth; we can clarify or obscure the vision they have set for their future. And we can do all of these things with just a few words. That's because we know the truth about them. We see their weaknesses and, if we're not careful, we can use that knowledge to their detriment. But if we are willing, we can know a greater truth—God's truth—that encourages them in who they are and what their future holds. Love always chooses God's truth.

"IF YOU LOVE SOMEONE, YOU WILL ALWAYS BE LOYAL TO HIM NO MATTER WHAT THE COST. YOU WILL ALWAYS BELIEVE IN HIM, ALWAYS EXPECT THE BEST OF HIM, AND ALWAYS STAND YOUR GROUND IN DEFENDING HIM."

It was a difficult time in our home. My husband had been very irritable and depressed all week, and I was relieved when I didn't have to be around him. Although he had recently experienced some major setbacks in his work and hurtful disappointments in some of his personal and business relationships, I didn't feel that those were adequate justifications for him to take out his frustrations on me. As I thoroughly rehearsed a confrontation speech in my mind, he came into the room where I was working and sat down.

What now? I thought, looking at him keenly with one raised eyebrow and no hint of a smile. I prepared myself for the worst.

"I feel like my life is finished," he said. "I don't know if these disasters are temporary or a sign of things to come, but it's like starting all over again. And I don't think I have the strength anymore."

He waited for me to say something. As I mentally ran through the highlights of my previously rehearsed lecture, I knew I had been given the opportunity to set the tone for the future days, weeks, and perhaps even years of our lives. Would I speak the truth as I saw it, or would I speak the truth from God's perspective? It was a moment of struggle for me.

"God, what *is* Your truth about this situation?" I silently prayed. "What are *You* wanting to say to Michael through all that is going on in his life?"

In an instant I saw my husband as a young son—not mine, but God's. And instead of seeing his shortcomings, I saw his future. I saw his potential and all the gifts God had given him.

"You're not seeing straight," I finally said. "You're seeing through the eyes of the flesh, and God wants you to see through the eyes of the Spirit. Your life's not over; it's beginning. God didn't put all these gifts in you only to leave you with nothing and put you out to pasture. He just wants to get your attention because He desires to take you to the next step, and He prefers that you follow Him instead of trying to get there by yourself. If you will take God's hand, He will get you there. I know you can do it."

 I had never before realized that hope has a look. And at that moment I saw hope come over my husband's face. The words of encouragement I spoke probably didn't last longer than thirty seconds, but it was apparent that his life was now set on a different course. That's because the words I spoke weren't mine; they were God's. They were the kind of words that make chimes ring in the soul—a reverberation that is heard when truth penetrates the stronghold of a lie. I was grateful that I had resisted speaking the words *I* had prepared. I know now that they would have deepened the hurt in his heart and established a chasm

between us. They were my truth for a moment, but they weren't the ultimate truth for his life. God held the truth that brought joy to us both.

Love is
being there
sensing a need
seeing into another's soul
not betraying a confidence
overlooking a transgression
sharing yourself with someone else
encouraging a person to be all they can be

Knowledge puffs up, but love builds up.

—1 Corinthians 8:1 NIV

Love is very patient and kind,

never jealous or envious, never boastful or

proud, never haughty or selfish or rude.

Love does not demand its own way.

It is not irritable or touchy.

It does not hold grudges and will hardly even

notice when others do wrong.

It is never glad about injustice,

but rejoices whenever truth wins out.

If you love someone, you will always be loyal to him,

no matter what the cost.

You will always believe in him,

always expect the best of him,

and always stand your ground in defending him.

All the special gifts and powers from God

will someday come to an end, but love goes on forever.

—1 Corinthians 13:4-8

$\mathcal{L}ove$
Never Fails

$\mathcal{T}$he only love that never fails is God's love. Although we try to do our best to show love one simple act, gesture, or word at a time, we're still made of clay. And we still have times when we are too tired, too lazy, too blind, too preoccupied, or too human to show love perfectly.

But there is one foolproof act of love that always works. It always delivers and always accomplishes. It is always felt, even if the recipient can't identify exactly what it is. That is the act of praying. When we pray for someone else, we are in effect sending the love of God to penetrate that person's entire life.

So if we want to show unfailing love, prayer is the best place to start. That's because God is love, and God never fails. Therefore, when God is in it, love never fails either.